Awakenings

Barbara Rennick, B.A., M.Ed.
Principal
Halton Board of Education

Milree Armstrong, B.A., M.Ed.
Principal
Halton Board of Education

Margaret Deeth, B.A., A.T.C.M.
Coordinator, Early Childhood Education
Toronto Board of Education

Barbara Sutherland, B.A.
Consultant, Early Childhood Development Program
East York Board of Education

McGraw-Hill Ryerson Limited

Toronto, Montréal, New York, St. Louis, San Francisco, Auckland, Bogotá,
Guatemala, Hamburg, Johannesburg, Lisbon, London, Madrid, Mexico,
New Delhi, Panama, Paris, San Juan, São Paulo, Singapore, Sydney, Tokyo

Awakenings

ISBN 0-07-077917-1

1 2 3 4 5 6 7 8 9 0   SM   3 2 1 0 9 8 7 6 5 4

Printed and bound in Canada.

Designer: Elaine Macpherson

Illustrators:

Ron Berg, 36
Victoria Birta, 7, 12-27, 46-48, 79
Sarah Jane English, 38, 83, 87-90
Laszlo Gal, 65-74
Edward Gorey, 63
Sarie Jenkins, 85, 92-103
Tibor Kovalik, 104-109
Elaine Macpherson, 39-44
Helen Mason, 80-81
Jock MacRae, 8-10, 37, 50-61
Barbara Reid, 29-34

Canadian Cataloguing in Publication Data

Main entry under title:
Awakenings

(Unicorn, a reading and language series)
ISBN 0-07-077917-1

1. Readers (Primary). 2. Readers — 1950—
I. Rennick, Barbara. II. Series.

PE1119.A92 1984   428.6   C83-098823-8

Awakenings

Table of Contents

UNIT 1
Shivering in My Shoes

The Longest Journey in the World

"Last one into bed
has to switch out the light."
It's just the same every night.
There's a race.
I'm ripping off my trousers and shirt,
he's kicking off his shoes and socks.

"My sleeve's stuck."
"This button's too big for its buttonhole."
"Have you hidden my pyjamas?"
"Keep your hands off mine."

If you win
you get where it's safe
before the darkness comes —
but if you lose,
if you're last,
you know what you've got coming up is
the journey from the light switch to your bed.
It's the Longest Journey in the World.

"You're last tonight," my brother says.
And he's right.

There is nowhere so dark
as that room in the moment
after I've switched out the light.

There is nowhere so full of dangerous things,
things that love dark places,
things that breathe only when you breathe
and hold their breath when I hold mine.

So I have to say:
"I'm not scared."
That face, grinning in the pattern on the wall,
isn't a face —
"I'm not scared."
That prickle on the back of my neck
is only the label on my pyjama jacket —
"I'm not scared."
That moaning-moaning is nothing
but water in a pipe —
"I'm not scared."

Everything's going to be just fine
as soon as I get into that bed of mine.
Such a terrible shame
it's always the same;
it takes so long
it takes so long
it takes so long
to get there.

From the light switch
to my bed
it's the Longest Journey in the World.

Michael Rosen

The Climb

The sign was marked BEGINNERS' TRAIL.

"Are we going up there?" Brendan asked, squinting at the mountain that rose above the forest ahead. At the top was a great brow of rock, sprinkled with dark, stunted trees.

His cousin Nora nodded.

"Not me," said Brendan. "I don't want to."

"Don't be scared. It's easy," Nora coaxed. "See, the sign says it's for beginners. People go up all the time. It's really great!"

"I'm not scared," Brendan mumbled, looking at his feet. "I just don't want to."

"What a baby," Nora said to herself. Brendan was four years younger than Nora, but she thought he acted even younger. He had come with Aunt Barbara for the weekend, and Nora was supposed to entertain him.

Nora had wanted to rock on the cool farmhouse porch and listen to the women talk. Instead, Mother had packed a lunch and told her to take her cousin on a picnic.

"Come on, Bren, we'll just climb a little way up, and then we'll have lunch," Nora said.

Waves of heat pressed against them as they walked through the field, and grasshoppers shot across their path like sparks.

"I'm so sweaty," Brendan whined. "And I'm thirsty." He eyed the thermos sticking out of Nora's pack.

"But we just started," Nora said with annoyance.

When they entered the cool, damp forest Brendan stopped complaining. Its silence seemed to work a spell on him.

"You can be the trail guide," Nora said so Brendan would feel important.

He ran ahead to discover each rock and tree that was marked with red paint, until he came to the solid wall of the mountain that rose almost straight up. He turned and looked at Nora.

"Just follow the red markers," Nora said.

Tree roots formed natural steps up the huge boulders piled along the base of the mountain. As the trail grew steep the children clung to the trees. The path was spongy with fallen needles.

"It smells like Christmas," Brendan said.

Then there was nothing ahead but the broad brow of pitted grey rock that they had seen near the top of the mountain. There were no footholds and nothing to grab onto.

"What do we do now?" Brendan asked.

Nora grinned. Without answering, she walked right up the slope and then turned back.

"See, it's easy."

"You said we would stop if I wanted to," Brendan whimpered. "I want to go home now."

"Okay. Go home, baby," Nora taunted. "But I'm having the picnic. We're almost there."

Brendan hesitated and then started slowly, cautiously up the rock.

"Faster. You've got to walk faster," Nora urged. "Don't stop!"

But Brendan wavered. His breath was coming in hoarse gasps. He felt the pull backwards and almost lost his balance. He dropped to his hands and knees a few metres from where Nora waited.

"Nora!" Brendan pleaded. "Help me!" He pressed his face to the rough stone and looked down to the valley below. It began to roll before his eyes, making him feel sick. "Nora, I'm going to fall! I'm afraid!"

"Don't look down, Brendan. Look at me." Nora held out her hand to Brendan. She could see he was really frightened. "Look at me, Brendan," she said firmly. "You're not going to fall. You're going to walk up as easy as pie."

Slowly Brendan crawled up, his eyes never leaving Nora's outstretched hand. When he reached her, she pulled him to his feet. From there on, the slope was more gradual, and together they walked the short distance to the top. Brendan laughed nervously as he felt how well his rubber soles gripped the rock.

Nora sat down and laid out the picnic.

"Look, Nora," Brendan pointed. "There's your house. I wonder if they can see us up here."

Below them in the valley, Nora's house, the barn, the trees, and even the cows in their bright field looked like tiny toys. Behind the valley marched row after row of mountains, each looking as if it were cut from cardboard. Those farthest away grew fainter and fainter, until the last ones dissolved into the sky.

Nora and Brendan ate their lunch. Then they stretched out lazily on the warm rock and watched a distant hawk rise screeching on the updrafts of air.

Nora stuffed the lunch wrappers in her sack and stood up. "I've got something else to show you, Brendan."

A red arrow on the rock pointed to a wooded path that wound around the top of the mountain. The trees here grew slowly and were twisted by the wind. The trail soon crossed over a small cave formed by a rock slab balanced on several others.

Brendan had to bend down to peer inside. "Does anything live in there?" he asked.

"Bears, probably," Nora answered.

Brendan jumped back.

"Don't worry," Nora said. "They sleep during the day."

"Is this what you wanted to show me?" Brendan asked.

"No. There's something even better," Nora said. "Come on."

The shadowy path snaked around and between more boulders, but the hard climbing part was over. After a while the forest opened on all sides to blue sky, and their trail ended again upon bare rock. Nora steadied Brendan as he followed the last arrow up to the topmost jut of rock.

"Boy!" Brendan shouted. "This must be the top of the world!"

It was not their familiar world of houses and small farms that was mirrored in the lake below them. It was a world of low mountains furred with trees like the backs of sleeping animals.

"Didn't I tell you it was great?" Nora asked.

But Brendan ignored her question.

"Don't you wish you could ride on those shadows?" he asked. He was watching the shadows cast by the clouds slide across the slopes like magic carpets.

On the way back Brendan forgot his fear of the mountain. Every time Nora pointed out one of the trail markers, he would look annoyed and say, "I saw it already." And if she tried to help him over a difficult place, he would brush her aside, saying confidently, "I can do it myself."

"Hey, Bren," she said with excitement as she perched on a tree that had fallen across the path. "I've got a great idea for a game. I'll go ahead to the big rock where we ate lunch and wait for you. Pretend that I'm lost. You be the search party and find me. Okay?" She tried hard not to smile and make him suspicious.

Brendan's face lit up. "Yeah! I'll count up to fifty, and then I'll come find you," he agreed.

He turned his back on her and covered his eyes, counting aloud, "One, two, three, four . . ."

Nora raced ahead until she came to the cave. It was smaller than she remembered. Maybe there is something in there, she thought. But she couldn't waste time wondering. Brendan's footsteps were already thudding down the path. He couldn't have counted to fifty.

When she scrambled inside on her hands and knees, she found it wasn't really a cave. It was a rock tunnel with straight sides almost as narrow as her body, like the Egyptian tomb she had seen at the museum. The ceiling became so low that she had to wriggle along on her elbows, pushing at the soft dirt floor with her toes. Brendan's footsteps were overhead now. She squeezed back as far as she could so he wouldn't be able to see her.

She tried an experimental growl. "Rrrrah!" It echoed from the rock walls. "Grrraah!" she growled louder, enjoying how deep her voice sounded. "Grrraah, rrrahrrah!" she added for good measure and bit her lip to keep from laughing.

She listened. Everything was quiet. She could imagine Brendan running for dear life. She laughed out loud. Then she was aware of the mouldy odour in the cave. It smelled of earth and rotting wood, like the crawl space under the house where creepy things scurried. She couldn't see very well now because her body blocked most of the light coming in from the entrance.

Maybe I'd better go after Brendan, she thought. He'll tell Mother on me. Or maybe he's lost the trail.

She straightened her arms to back out, banging her head hard against the roof of the cave. "Ow!" She lowered her shoulders, but as she bent her knees to crawl, the rough stone scraped the skin over her backbone where her shirt had ridden up. She couldn't get out!

"I've got to get out!" she yelled. "I want to go home!"

Brendan had said the same thing when he was afraid of falling. He must be waiting for her on the rock, Nora thought. Or maybe he had started home without her. She groaned. Brendan didn't even know where she was.

"Brendan," she pleaded out loud. "Oh Brendan, please come back!"

"Nora? Are you in the cave, Nora?" a small voice asked. "What's the matter?"

Nora started. Had she really heard it, Brendan's voice? And so near!

"Brendan! I can't get out of here," Nora called.

"Did you get stuck?" he asked. "I can see your feet."

If Brendan could see her, she couldn't be far from the outside. She could get out if she tried. Nora didn't feel alone any more, cut off from the rest of the world. The world was close, as close as Brendan's voice.

Slowly, awkwardly she wriggled out the way she had come in. It was much harder going backwards, but she was calm now, and she knew she could do it.

"Boy, you're all dirty," Brendan observed as she stood up and brushed herself off. "And you hurt your face!"

The concern on his face made Nora feel ashamed. "I'm sorry if I scared you when I growled," she said.

"That's okay," he answered. "You didn't scare me. I knew it was you all the time."

The climb down went quickly. They felt as if the earth were pulling them toward the bottom of the mountain, and the muscles in their legs trembled from the strain. Brendan said nothing when they reached the bare rock face, but he placed his feet carefully and clung tightly to Nora's hand.

Soon they were on the almost flat part of the trail through the forest. Brendan was chattering happily now, and Nora pointed out the woodpecker's tree and a squirrel's nest.

Suddenly there was a loud squeal behind them. They both screamed. As Nora turned to look, there was another smaller squeak.

"Oh!" She laughed with relief. "See that tree leaning against the other one? When the wind moves them, their bark rubs together. Did that scare you?"

"At first," Brendan admitted.

"It scared me, too," said Nora.

Brendan waited until they were out of the forest and walking across the field to ask, "Nora, could we go up the mountain again tomorrow?"

"Sure," Nora answered, giving her cousin a squeeze. "Only this time you hide, and I'll look for you."

Carol Carrick

I Whistle a Happy Tune

Words by Oscar Hammerstein II
Music by Richard Rodgers

When - ev - er I feel a - fraid, I hold my head e - rect And whis - tle a hap - py tune So no one will sus - pect I'm a - fraid._____ While shiv - er - ing in my shoes, I strike a care - less pose And whis - tle a hap - py tune And no one ev - er knows I'm a - fraid._____ The re - sult of this de - cep - tion Is ve - ry strange to___ tell, For when I fool the

peo-ple I fear, I fool my-self as well. I whis-tle a hap-py tune And ev-ery sin-gle time, The hap-pi-ness in the tune Con-vin-ces me that I'm not a-fraid.

"I Whistle a Happy Tune" (from musical 'The King and I'). (Music: Richard Rodgers/Lyrics: Oscar Hammerstein II). © 1951 by Richard Rodgers and Oscar Hammerstein II. Copyright renewed. Williamson Music Inc. owner of publication and allied rights. Used by permission.

Anna, Grandpa, and the Big Storm

Anna looked at her rosy-cheeked grandfather. Snow clung to his moustache and eyebrows and froze. They looked like tiny icebergs.

"Here comes the train!" Grandpa shouted.

A steam engine, pulling two green cars, puffed toward them. When the train stopped, Anna and Grandpa hurried across the platform and stepped inside. There were lots of empty seats.

Anna pulled off her hat. Her pom-pom looked like a big white snowball. She shook it, spraying the floor with wet snow. The conductor came up the aisle and stopped at their seat.

"That will be five cents," the conductor said. "Each."

"You mean I have to pay for her, too?" Grandpa's eyes twinkled.

"Grandpa," Anna whispered, tugging at his arm, "I'm almost eight years old."

Grandpa and the conductor laughed. Anna didn't like to be teased. She turned away and tried to look out, but snow covered the windows.

Grandpa leaned forward. "Quite a storm," he said to the woman in the seat in front of them. "Nothing like the Blizzard of '72 though. Why it was so cold, the smoke froze as it came out of the chimney!"

The woman in the seat ahead turned around. "This storm can't last. First day of spring is less than two weeks away."

"That's just what I was telling my daughter this morning!" Grandpa said.

Suddenly the train stopped.

"What's the trouble?" a woman asked. "Conductor, why has the train stopped?"

The conductor didn't reply. He opened the car door and stepped out onto the platform. No one inside said a word.

Then Grandpa stood up. "I'll find out what's the matter."

Anna tugged at his coat sleeve. "Oh, please sit down,

Grandpa." He didn't seem to understand how scared she felt. How she wished she had stayed home!

The door opened again, and the conductor entered the car. He was covered with snow. "We're stuck," he said. "The engine can't move. Too much snow has drifted onto the tracks ahead. We'll have to stay here until help comes."

"Did you hear that, Anna?" Grandpa almost bounced up and down in his seat. "We're stuck! Stuck and stranded on the Third Avenue El! What do you think about that!"

When Anna heard the news, she grew even more frightened. "Mama will be so worried. She doesn't know where we are."

"She knows you are with me," Grandpa said cheerfully. "That's all she needs to know." He leaned forward again. "We might as well get acquainted," he said. "My name is Erik Jensen, and this is my granddaughter, Anna."

The woman in the seat ahead turned around. "Josie Sweeney," she said. "Pleased to meet you."

"How-dee-do," said the woman across the aisle. "I'm Mrs. Esther Polanski. And this is my friend, Miss Ruth Cohen."

Someone tapped Anna on her shoulder. She turned around. Two young men smiled. One man said, "John King and my brother Bruce."

A young woman with a high fur collar and a big hat sat by herself at the rear of the car. Anna looked in her direction. "My name is Anna Romano," she said shyly.

"I'm Addie Beaver," said the young woman. She smiled and wrapped her coat more tightly around her.

It was growing colder and colder inside the car. When the conductor shook the snow off his clothes, it no longer melted into puddles on the floor.

"We'll all freeze to death if we stay here," moaned Mrs. Sweeney.

"Oooooo, my feet are so cold," Addie Beaver said.

Anna looked at her high-button shoes and felt sorry for Addie

Beaver. Even though Anna had on her warm boots, her toes began to grow cold, too. She stood in the aisle and stamped her feet up and down.

Suddenly Anna had an idea. "Grandpa!" she said. "I know a game we can play that might help keep us warm."

"Why Anna, what a good idea," Grandpa replied.

"It's called 'Simon Says.'"

"Listen everybody!" Grandpa shouted. "My granddaughter, Anna, knows a game that will help us stay warm."

"How do we play, Anna?" asked Mrs. Polanski. "Tell us."

"Everybody has to stand up," said Anna.

"Come on, everybody," Grandpa said. "We must keep moving if we don't want to freeze to death."

Miss Beaver was the first to stand. Then John and Bruce King stood up. Grandpa bowed first to Mrs. Sweeney, then to Mrs. Polanski and Miss Cohen. "May I help you ladies?" he asked. They giggled and stood up. Now everybody was looking at Anna.

"All right," she said. "You must do only what Simon tells you to do. If *I* tell you to do something, you mustn't do it."

"I don't understand," Mrs. Sweeney said.

"Maybe we'll catch on if we start playing," Grandpa said.

"All right," Anna said. "I'll begin. Simon says, 'Clap your hands.'"

Everybody began to clap hands.

"Simon says, 'Stop!'"

Everybody stopped.

"Good!" Anna said. "Simon says, 'Follow me!'" Anna marched down the aisle of the car, then around one of the poles, then back again. Everyone followed her.

"Simon says, 'Stop!'"

Everyone stopped.

Anna patted her head and rubbed her stomach at the same time. "Simon says, 'Pat your head and rub your stomach.' Like this."

Everyone began to laugh at one another.

"Simon says, 'Swing your arms around and around.'"

"Ooof! This is hard work!" puffed Mrs. Sweeney.

"Now. Touch your toes!"

Mrs. Sweeney bent down and tried to touch her toes.

"Oh, oh! You're out, Mrs. Sweeney!" Anna said.

"Why am I out?" she asked indignantly.

Anna giggled. "Because *Simon* didn't say to touch your toes; *I* did!"

Mrs. Sweeney sat down. "It's just as well," she panted. "I was getting all tired out."

"Is everyone warming up?" Grandpa asked.

"Yes! Yes!" they all shouted.

Snow was sifting like flour through the cracks around the windows. Just then, the door opened. A blast of icy cold air blew into the car. Everyone shivered. It was the conductor coming back in again.

"Get ready to leave," he said. "The firefighters are coming!"

Carla Stevens

To find out how the firefighters rescued everyone, read *Anna, Grandpa, and the Big Storm* by Carla Stevens.

Snow Today

The weatherman said, "Snow today,"
but children gazed in vain
for frosty snowflakes to be seen
beyond the window pane.

The weatherman said, "Snow tonight,
get out long underwear!"
But even though the children hoped,
the morning ground was bare.

The weatherman said, "Sun all day,
and clear until the dark."
By noon the sky was thick with snow
as winter left its mark!

Fran Newman

UNIT 2
Cat Tales

This Cat

This cat
Walks into the room and across the floor,
Under a chair, around the bed,
Behind the table, and out the door.
I'm sitting on the chair,
And I don't see where he is.
I don't see one hair of his.
I just hear the floorboards scarcely squeak.
This cat comes and goes
On invisible toes.
The sneak.

Karla Kuskin

Jenny's Adopted Brothers

The little black cat, Jenny Linsky, sat down beside the rose-bush in her master's garden. The roses were in bloom, the birds were singing, and the sun shone brightly.

"How lucky I am to have this garden and a master like the Captain," thought Jenny. "I wish every cat could have the nice things I have."

At that moment, Jenny was surprised to see a black and white cat sitting alone in a corner of the garden.

"There's a cat I've never seen before," continued Jenny. "He looks as if he wants something. He's bigger than I, but maybe I can help him."

Jenny straightened the red scarf she was wearing and ran over to the stranger.

"Hello," she said. "My name is Jenny Linsky. What's yours?"

The stranger removed a red ball he was holding in his mouth and said, "My name is Checkers."

"Checkers what?" asked Jenny.

"I can't remember my last name," said Checkers. "So much has happened that I've forgotten lots of things."

"Checkers is a very pretty name," said Jenny in a comforting voice. "And it's a good name for you," she added as she examined the furry, black checks on his thin, white legs. "But you look hungry. Don't they feed you at home?"

"I haven't any home," said Checkers.

"No home?" cried Jenny. "Oh, it isn't fair! Why, Checkers, I have this lovely garden and that brick house with the ivy on it. And my master, Captain Tinker, is the nicest master in the world."

As she gazed at Checkers' darling, heart-shaped face, she had a bright idea.

"Checkers," she said, "I'm Captain Tinker's only cat. If you'll come home with me, I'll ask the Captain to adopt you."

"Thank you," cried Checkers joyfully. "I'll go with you as soon as Edward comes."

"Edward? Who is he?" asked Jenny.

"Edward is my big brother," replied Checkers. "His last name is Brandywine. We met when both of us lost our homes, and we've been brothers ever since. Where I go, Edward goes too."

"Checkers," sighed Jenny, "maybe my master isn't rich enough to adopt two —"

Jenny didn't have time to finish her sentence. Edward had heard his name, and he came hurrying out of the bushes.

He was a tiger cat with a broad, white chest and beautiful eyes. But in those eyes, there was the sad look of cats who have no homes.

"Edward," said Checkers, "this is Jenny Linsky. She's going to ask her master, Captain Tinker, to adopt us."

Just then a bell rang in the garden.

"That's the Captain calling me to lunch," explained Jenny.

Checkers picked up his red ball and started toward the Captain's house.

40

But Jenny said, "Wait. It isn't easy to get *two* cats adopted. We must work out a plan."

She thought hard for a moment and then said, "I have it. I'll try to get you adopted one at a time."

"Jenny," begged Edward, "please try to get Checkers adopted first. He's smaller than I and very hungry. I'll wait outside your house until you call me. If you don't call me, I'll know the Captain hasn't enough room for me."

"Edward!"cried Checkers. "Didn't you and I promise to stick together?"

Edward gazed up toward the point where the tall buildings of the city scraped the sky. His right nostril twitched. "I smell a storm," he murmured. "By night we shall have rain."

Then he looked tenderly at Checkers and said, "Another night outdoors in the cold rain might make you sick. Please go with Jenny into Captain Tinker's house. Show him the retrieving trick I taught you. I'm sure he'll adopt you when he sees how nicely you retrieve."

"Retrieve? What's that?" asked Jenny.

"To retrieve means to run after something and bring it back,"

explained Checkers. "This red ball I carry everywhere is my
retrieving ball."

At that moment the lunch bell sounded for the second time.

"We mustn't keep the Captain waiting," said Jenny.
"Checkers, when we get home, you must retrieve for us."

The three cats ran toward Captain Tinker's house. On the
way Jenny asked Edward, "Can you retrieve too?"

"No," he answered. "There's no trick I can do. But some day,
if I find a home that has a little office in it, I should like to write."

"Write what?" asked Jenny.

"Write about the troubles I've had," replied Edward.

When the cats reached the house, Edward crawled into the
bushes near the open window, and Jenny led Checkers through
the window, into the living room.

Captain Tinker, who was an old sailor, was sitting in his
armchair, waiting for Jenny.

He must have been surprised to see her bringing home a
black and white cat, with a heart-shaped face, who held a red
ball in his mouth. But the Captain was polite to cats. He let
Jenny speak first.

She whispered to Checkers, "Retrieve."

Checkers passed his ball to Jenny. "Hit it hard," he said.

She batted it across the floor. He bounded after it, caught it with his teeth, returned with it, and laid it at the Captain's feet.

The Captain said to Checkers, "That was the most beautiful retrieving I've ever seen. And such a pretty ball!"

Checkers whispered to Jenny. "Hit the ball again. I must retrieve some more to help get Edward adopted."

But Captain Tinker picked up the ball and, looking thoughtfully at Checkers, said, "You're hungry, and a red ball never filled an empty stomach. You must stay and eat some lunch with Jenny. After that—why, after that, you may live with us forever, if you wish."

"Checkers," cried Jenny happily, "you've been adopted. Now I'll call Edward.

She turned toward the window. To her surprise, she saw that Edward had come to the window-sill without waiting to be called.

On his striped face there was a look that Jenny had never seen on any cat. It was the look of a cat gazing at something warm and beautiful which he may have to leave because he is not wanted.

"Oh!" thought Jenny. "The Captain mustn't send Edward away; it would break his heart. I must speak to the Captain about this and try to make him understand."

Jenny was on the point of jumping onto her master's knees to plead for Edward when the Captain caught sight of the face at the window. And he saw Checkers glance quickly at the face. Then Checkers sat very straight and still, like someone wishing hard for something to come true.

"These two cats belong together," murmured Captain Tinker. Without another word he walked to the window and pulled Edward gently into the room. In that way Edward was adopted.

Esther Averill

Tabitha Twitchell

Tabitha Twitchell was sleek and fat,
A pampered and petted Persian cat.
She lived in a beautiful country house
And never—no never—had seen a mouse.
Tabitha dined on chicken and fish
Served on a little china dish.
She slept at night in a soft, warm bed
With a fluffy pillow and pretty spread.

Tabitha never went outside,
But the rooms in her house were big and wide.
She had plenty of room to explore and roam,
Safe in her beautiful country home.

Now one dark night in the fall of the year,
Tabitha woke with a start to hear
A scritching, scratching kind of sound.
"What's that?" she thought. "There's no one around
To make a noise that sounds like that."
Tabitha Twitchell, sleek and fat,
Stretched and yawned and opened her eyes.
Then the Persian cat had quite a surprise.

There in a corner of the hall
Peeking out of a hole in the wall
She saw two ears, two eyes, and a nose
In a furry face. "Now I suppose
This creature has come to visit me,"
Thought Tabitha Twitchell, calm as can be.

"Hello," she mewed. "Have you come to play?
I'd rather you waited till break of day.
I'm sleepy now and I need my rest.
Come back tomorrow, that will be best."
The visitor blinked and looked at the cat.
"My whiskers!" he thought. "Just look at that!
I do believe that the cat in this house
Has never before seen a country mouse."

"You're supposed to chase me," the mouse replied.
"But *you* couldn't catch a mouse if you tried.
You're much too lazy and much too fat.
I'm not afraid of a pampered cat!"

Tabitha Twitchell yawned once more
And looked at the mouse. "Never before
Have I seen a mouse in this house," she said.
"Now run along. My soft, warm bed
Is much too comfortable, I admit.
I have no intentions of leaving it."

"Then you'll let me stay?" asked the little mouse.
"You'll let me live in your beautiful house?
I like it a lot. It's just right, you know,
And I really have nowhere else to go."

"You may stay," said Tabitha, "if you wish.
I'll let you share my chicken and fish,
For to tell the truth it's lonely here
With no other furry creatures near."

So that is the story of one fine cat
With a mouse for a friend, and that is that!
The two became friends, and the country house
Now belongs to a cat — and a *pampered mouse!*

Jean Conder Soule

The Climbing Cat

"Mom!" cried Richie. "He isn't back yet. I thought he'd be here this morning. You said . . ."

Richie stood as close as he dared to the big black stove. He felt like a marshmallow held over a coal — one side cold, one side nearly burned. Daddy had known how to haul this chunky stove all the way up the mountain to the mine — and the big tin bathtub, too. If he could haul big things up a tall mountain, he could probably figure out some way to haul a little cat down from a tall tree. But Richie was worried anyway.

"Black Cat has been up that fir tree a whole day and night. And Paul McGee says he can feel snow coming. He says he can tell by his bones. I think I'll go over to the cookhouse and see if Black Cat's there. He might have come down last night. I bet he's sitting on Paul McGee's woodbox right now."

"Well . . .," said his mother. "Oh well, all right. But put on your heavy coat. There was some snow last night."

Snow! Black Cat was a summer kitten — he didn't even know what snow was or how it could sting you and slap you and push you and cover you.

It was not far from the cabin to the cookhouse. Richie ran, his feet stumbling on the frozen ground. There was not much snow — just a dusting really, as if some careless giant cook had sifted a little flour down the mountainside. But more snow would come. Paul McGee's aching bones said so. The frowning grey sky said so.

There were three signs on the door of the big log cookhouse. The top one, in large red letters, said:

MOON TREE MINING COMPANY

50

Beneath it a smaller sign, in neat black letters, said:

COOKHOUSE

And the biggest sign of all, made of dirty cardboard, and lettered carefully in dark blue crayon, said:

PAUL McGEE COOK

Inside was Paul McGee, stirring a large pot of porridge for the men, who sat along the scrubbed board table, looking hungry. Paul McGee's round, red face smiled at Richie. Sam and Mike and Swede and the others called out and grinned their welcome.

Richie hardly noticed. He looked at the woodbox by the stove. Then he looked under the stove and under the table.

"He's not here, kid," said Mike. "When I came up from Number Four this morning, I saw him still way up that big fir. I didn't know a cat could get up that high. I don't blame him if he doesn't want to come down."

Paul McGee said, "Have some porridge, Richie. Good for the stomach on a cold day."

"Thank you, Paul McGee, but I'm not hungry. I think I'll go over and call Black Cat again. Maybe if he sees I'm wearing my heavy coat, he'll know more snow is coming and come down."

"That cat knows snow is coming after sitting up there in the cold all night," said Mike. He speared a slice of toast with his fork and dumped a large spoonful of strawberry jam on it. "He's just too scared to come down. Probably chased one of those cheeky bluejays clean up the tree. Then the old bluejay flew away laughing and left Black Cat up there looking down, scared stiff."

52

"Black Cat's not scared; he's just stubborn. Mom says he'll come down. If he doesn't, Daddy will think of some way to get him down when he gets back," Richie told Mike.

"Your dad won't be back in camp for about three more days," said Mike.

"Eat your toast before it gets cold, and don't talk so much, Mike," Paul McGee said.

When Richie reached the tall fir tree, he suddenly felt very small. This was a real moon tree. The moon would have to watch out going past here; the tip of this tree really scratched the sky. And there was Black Cat, so far up in the thin tangled top branches that he seemed to be more like a furry black caterpillar than a cat.

"Come on down, kitty, kitty. It's going to snow. Come on, kitty, kitty, kitty," Richie called. He thought that Black Cat meowed in reply, but it might have been the wind.

"Of all trees on Moontree Mountain, your cat sure picked the grand-daddy of them all to climb," said a voice.

Richie turned, startled to see Paul McGee standing beside him.

"I got to thinking," continued Paul McGee. "Maybe if Black Cat smells dinner, his very favourite dinner, he'll get over his scare and come down."

He held out his hand. In it was a large open tin of salmon, juicy and pink.

"Let's leave him alone now, and let that salmon do the trick," suggested Paul McGee, placing the tin carefully under the tree. "No cat could turn down a feed like that. Bet he's down by this time tomorrow, licking his chops and looking for more."

But next morning Black Cat was still up the tree. The salmon was frozen into a hard, pink lump.

"I guess he wasn't hungry enough," said Paul McGee.

"He looks hungry," said Richie, "and tired and cold. Mike's right, Black Cat is scared. Oh, I wish Daddy were home!"

"If food won't bring him down," said Paul McGee doubtfully, "then I don't know what will."

Mike and Sam and Swede came clumping along. They all stood craning their necks, looking at Black Cat.

"Climb up!" cried Richie.

"Too dangerous, even with lumbermen's rigging, which we don't have," said Paul McGee. "Half those top branches are rotten — couldn't risk it."

"Have to shoot him," said Mike. "Can't let the animal freeze to death."

"No, please don't do that!" cried Richie. "Don't shoot him!"

Paul McGee said thoughtfully, "You know, maybe we could make a sort of ladder. We could fell one of those smaller trees over there," he pointed, "and lean it into the big fir. Maybe if Black Cat had a slanty way down, instead of straight down, he might just try it."

"Let's do it, let's do it!" cried Richie.

The men spent a great deal of time picking the right tree to fell. They licked their forefingers and held them up to test the wind. The wind was cold, and it whispered, "Snow coming,

snow coming." They measured distances by pacing out big steps with their big boots.

"This is the one," said Paul McGee at last.

The men set to work with axe and saw, and soon Paul McGee cried, "Timber!"

Richie shut his eyes tight. When he opened them again, there was the small tree slanted cosily into the tall fir. It did make a sort of ladder. But Black Cat had climbed farther up the tree. Now he was balanced on a very small branch, and he arched his back, hissing weakly. No matter how much they called and coaxed, Black Cat would not come down from the tree.

When he woke the next morning, Richie knew right away what had happened. He could tell by the strange white light in his room and the piping of white around his window pane.

The snow had come. He just didn't want to go over to the tall fir tree. It would be draped in heavy white. Nothing small and black could be in that tree now.

He was surprised to see Paul McGee and Mike standing beneath the tree.

"That cat is still up there," said Paul McGee. "He's tough, like all of us on Moontree Mountain. But he has been up that tree for more than three days now. He's got the wobbles, and he won't last in all this snow. Mike here thinks we should shoot him."

"Can't let him freeze to death," said Mike.

"Coaxing and calling didn't work, canned salmon didn't work, and making a ladder didn't work. There just isn't anything else we can do," added Paul McGee.

"Yes there is!" cried Richie. "Yes there is! No one is going to shoot Black Cat, not my Black Cat!"

He started to run toward the tool shed. Twice he fell. The snow became packed up his coat sleeves and down inside his boots.

"Richie, what are you doing?" exclaimed his mother, as he puffed and stumbled back to the tree. He was dragging the big double-bladed axe behind him.

"I'm going to cut down the tree!" yelled Richie. "That's how I'm going to get him down!"

"You can't do that," said Paul McGee. "The fall will kill him."

"Yes I can. It's better than shooting him. At least he has a chance this way. At least I'm trying," Richie said fiercely. He could lift the axe only as high as his knees, but he swung it anyway with all his strength. It twisted awkwardly out of his hands and buried itself in the snow. Richie wondered if he were going to cry.

"Still say I should shoot him," said Mike, hunting in the snow for the axe. "But I'll tell Sam and Swede we have another wood-chopping job. I've always said I'd rather be a lumberjack than a miner anyway."

Sam and Swede each grasped an end of the whipping, whanging crosscut saw. They braced themselves, feet apart, and placed the sharp saw teeth against the thick bark. Sam pushed, Swede pulled, Sam pulled, Swede pushed, and in a

rasping rhythm the saw slowly sliced into the tree. Then they stood back, and Mike swung the heavy axe — *chop, thump, chop, thump* — cutting out a wedge of yellow wood. Then Sam and Swede scrambled around to the other side of the tree and once more began to saw. Perspiration rolled down their faces. The sawdust flew and piled up like yellow snow.

Black Cat peered down from his perch, trembling and shivering.

"It's going to go! Timber-r-r-r!" called Paul McGee.

The tree shuddered and groaned. It hesitated as though afraid and then, with a slow crackling roar, began to fall.

"Hang on, ride it down," Richie yelled. But what if Black Cat was on the *underside* of that falling green and white blur? He'd be crushed!

"Jump, jump, jump, jump!" Richie cried.

Something small and black shot from the tree. The fir crashed in a shower of flying snow, bounced with a thud that made Richie's stomach quiver, and then lay still, its branches waving and dipping.

A small black head poked out of the snow.

"Hurray!" howled Paul McGee, jumping up and down. He whacked Richie on the back; Swede shook hands with Sam; Sam shook hands with Mom; Mike shook hands with Paul McGee; and Mom kissed Richie.

Richie snatched Black Cat up and brushed the snow from his fur. No broken bones. He looked thin and a bit ashamed of himself, but he was safe. Black Cat started to purr a scratchy purr and rubbed his pointed face against Richie's cheek.

Richie forgot to feel cold. He felt warm — inside and outside and all over.

Margaret Coe

Chang McTang McQuarter Cat

Chang McTang McQuarter Cat
Is one part this and one part that.
One part is yowl, one part is purr.
One part is scratch, one part is fur.
One part, maybe even two,
Is how he sits and stares right through
You and you and you and you.
And when you feel my Chang-Cat stare,
You wonder if you're really there.

Chang McTang McQuarter Cat
Is one part this and ten parts that.
He's one part saint, and two parts sin,
One part yawn, and three parts grin,
One part sleepy, four parts lightning,
One part cuddly, five parts fright'ning,
One part snarl, and six parts play.
One part is how he goes away
Inside himself, somewhere miles back
Behind his eyes, somewhere as black
And green and yellow as the night
A jungle makes in full moonlight.

Chang McTang McQuarter Cat
Is one part this and twenty that.
One part is statue, one part tricks —
(One part, or six, or thirty-six.)

One part (or twelve, or sixty-three)
Is — Chang McTang belongs to ME!
Don't ask, "How many parts is that?"
Addition's nothing to a cat.

If you knew Chang, then you'd know this:
He's one part everything there is.

John Ciardi

UNIT 3
Awakenings

Pettranella

Long ago in a country far away lived a little girl named Pettranella. She lived with her father and mother in the upstairs of her grandmother's tall, narrow house.

Other houses just like it lined the street. At the end of the street was the mill. All day and all night smoke rose from its great smokestacks and lay like a grey blanket over the city. It hid the sun and choked the trees. It withered the flowers that tried to grow in the window-boxes.

One dark winter night when the wind blew cold from the east, Pettranella's father came home with a letter. The family gathered around the table in the warm yellow circle of the lamp to read it. Even the grandmother came from her rooms downstairs to listen.

"It's from Uncle Gus in Canada," began her father. "He has his homestead there now and is already clearing his land. Someday it will be a large farm growing many crops of grain." And then he read the letter aloud.

When he had finished, Pettranella said, "I wish we could go
there, too, and live on a homestead."

Her parents looked at each other, their eyes twinkling with a
secret. "We *are* going," said her mother. "We are sailing on the
very next ship."

Pettranella could hardly believe her ears. Suddenly she
thought of some things she had always wanted. "Can we have
some chickens?" she asked. "And a swing?"

"You will be in charge of the chickens," laughed her father,
"and I will put up a swing for you in our biggest tree."

"And Grandmother," cried Pettranella, "now you will have a
real flower garden, not just a window-box."

Pulling her close, the grandmother spoke gently. "I cannot go
to the new land with you, little one. I am too old to make such a
long journey."

Pettranella's eyes filled with tears. "Then I won't go either,"
she said.

But in the end, of course, she did.

When they were ready to leave, her grandmother gave her a small muslin bag. Pettranella opened it and looked inside. "There are seeds in here!" she exclaimed.

"There is a garden in there," said the old lady. "Those are flower seeds to plant when you get to your new home."

"Oh, I will take such good care of them," promised Pettranella. "And I will plant them and make a beautiful garden for you."

So they left their homeland. It was sad, thought Pettranella, but it was exciting, too. Sad to say good-bye to everyone they knew and exciting to be going across the ocean in a big ship.

At last they reached the shores of North America. As they stood at the rail waiting to leave the ship, she asked, "Can we see our homestead yet?"

Not yet, they told her. There was still a long way to go.

After many days, they came to a settlement where two rivers met. There they camped while the father got his homestead papers. Then they bought some things they would need:

an axe and a saw

a hammer and nails

sacks of food and seed

a plough and a cow and a strong brown ox

a cart with two large wooden wheels

some chickens

The ox was hitched to the cart. It was so full of all their belongings that there was barely room for Pettranella and her mother. Her father walked beside the ox, and the cow followed.

The wooden wheels creaked over the bumpy ground. At first Pettranella thought it was fun. Soon she began asking, "When are we going to get there?" and making rather a nuisance of herself climbing in and out of the cart.

Often at night, as they lay wrapped in their warm quilts beside the fire, they heard owls hooting and sometimes wolves calling to one another. Once they saw the northern lights.

One day, as they followed the winding trail through groves of spruce and poplar, there was a sudden *THUMP, CRACK, CRASH!*

"What happened?" cried Pettranella, as she slid off the cart into the mud.

"We have broken a shaft," said her father. "One of the wheels went over a big rock."

"Now we'll never find our homestead!" wailed Pettranella, as they began to unload the cart.

"We'll make a new shaft," said her father. Taking his axe, he went into the woods to cut a pole the right size.

Pettranella helped her mother make lunch, then sat down on a log to wait. Taking the bag of seeds from her pocket, she poured them out into a little pile on her lap. She thought all the while of the garden she would soon be making.

Just then she heard something. A familiar creaking and squeaking, and it was getting closer. It had to be — it was — another ox cart! "Somebody's coming!" she shouted, jumping up.

Her father came running out of the woods as the cart drew near. It was just like theirs, but the ox was black. The driver had a tanned, friendly face. When he saw their trouble, he swung down from his cart to help.

He helped the father make a new shaft. They fastened it in place and loaded the cart again.

Afterwards they all had lunch. Pettranella sat listening while the grown-ups talked together. Their new friend had a homestead near theirs, he said. He invited them to visit one day.

As they bumped along the trail, suddenly Pettranella thought about the flower seeds. She felt in her pocket, but there was nothing there. The muslin bag was gone!

"Oh, oh! Stop!" she cried. "The seeds are gone!"

71

Her father halted the ox. "I saw you looking at them before lunch," said her mother. "You must have spilled them there. You'll never find them now."

"I'm going back to look anyway," said Pettranella. Before they could stop her, she was running back down the trail.

She found the log, but she didn't find any seeds. Just the empty muslin bag.

As she trudged back to the cart, her tears began to fall. "I was going to make such a beautiful garden. Now I broke my promise to Grandmother!"

"Maybe you can make a vegetable garden instead," suggested her mother, but Pettranella knew it wouldn't be the same.

"I don't think turnips and cabbages are very pretty," she sighed.

It was later that afternoon, near teatime, when they found their homestead. Their own land, as far as they could see! Pettranella was so excited that for a while she forgot all about her lost seeds.

That night they slept on beds of spruce and tamarack boughs cut from their own trees. What a good smell, thought Pettranella, snuggling under her quilt.

The next morning her father began to put up a small cabin. Later he would build a larger one. Then he started to break the land. A small piece of ground was set aside for vegetables.

After it was dug, it was Pettranella's job to rake the earth and
gather the stones into a pile.

"Can we plant the seeds now?" she asked when she had
finished.

"Not yet," said her mother, "it's still too cold."

One morning they were awakened by a great noise that
filled the sky above them. "Wild geese!" shouted the father, as
they rushed outside to look. "They're on their way north. It's
really spring!"

Soon squirrels chattered and red-winged blackbirds sang. A
wobbly-legged calf was born to the cow, and sixteen baby
chicks hatched.

"Now we can plant the garden," said the mother, and they
did.

Early the next morning Pettranella ran outside to see if
anything had sprouted yet. The soil was bare; but a few days
later when she looked, she saw rows of tiny green shoots.

If only I hadn't lost Grandmother's seeds, she thought.
Flowers would be coming up now, too.

One warm Sunday a few weeks later, Pettranella put on a clean pinafore and her best sun-bonnet. She went to help her father hitch up the ox, for this was the day they were going to visit their neighbours.

As the ox cart bumped and bounced down the trail over which they had come so many weeks before, Pettranella thought about the little girl they were going to visit. She will probably be my very best friend, she thought to herself.

Suddenly her father stopped the cart and jumped down. "There's the rock where we broke the shaft," he said. "This time I will lead the ox around it."

"There's where we had lunch that day," said her mother.

"And there's the log I was sitting on when I lost the seeds," said Pettranella. "And look! LOOK AT ALL THOSE FLOWERS!"

There they were. Blowing gently in the breeze, their bright faces turned to the sun and their roots firm in the Canadian soil — Grandmother's flowers.

"Oh! Oh!" cried Pettranella, "I have never seen such beautiful flowers!"

Her mother's eyes were shining as she looked at them. "Just like the ones that grew in the countryside back home!" she exclaimed.

"You can plant them beside our house," said her father, "and make a flower garden there."

Pettranella did. She tended it carefully, and so her promise to her grandmother was not broken after all.

But she left some to grow beside the trail, that other settlers might see them and not feel lonely. To this very day, Pettranella's flowers bloom each year beside a country road in Manitoba.

Betty Waterton

I'm glad I don't live
Where it's sun and rain,
Then sun
And rain
Again, again!

I'm glad that I live
Where there's ice and snow,
And fall
And spring
And summer glow.

I'm glad that I live
Where seasons change;
I like
My world
To rearrange!

Fran Newman

It Must Be Spring

Words and music by Claire Senior Burke

Slowly

Deep in the heart of a ma - ple tree

Slow - ly the sap is stir - ring;

Up from the roots that reach far in the mud,

Up through the branch - es, out to the bud.

Quickly

"Oh!" says the tree, "I hear a rob - in sing! I'll

have to wake up for it must be spring!"

From **Songs and Silhouettes** by Claire Senior Burke. © Copyright 1933 by Gordon V. Thompson Limited, Toronto, Canada. Used by permission.

Sugaring Off

Drip, drip, drip
Sap from the maple tree.
The nights of frost and days of sun
Are here, and now the sap will run,
And sugaring off has just begun.

Run, run, run
Into the shiny pails.
The farmer's tapped the maple tree,
And maple sap is flowing free,
And brimming pails hang heavily.

Full, full, full
Then away to the sugar house
Where fires burn and leap and flare
While sap is boiling, bubbling clear,
And steaming fragrance fills the air.

Bubble, bubble, bubble
Then hurrah for the sugaring off!
The fire burns with a steady glow,
The paddle's stirring syrup-o,
And sugar's cooling on the snow.

Helen Guiton

Liquid Gold

When I arrived at my Uncle Dave's sugar bush early on a March morning, I found him getting ready to tap 80 large maples. Stacked outside his cabin were 150 pails and 150 taps — called "spiles" — waiting to be washed and sterilized.

I made the mistake of volunteering to clean the equipment. All that washing gave me dishpan hands.

To get at the sap, we would have to drill as many as three holes in each of the largest maples. A spile could then be hammered into each hole, and a pail would hang from the spile to catch the sap. Because it's possible to kill trees by drilling holes in them, my uncle showed me how to space the holes so they wouldn't be too harmful.

After making only 30 holes, my battery-operated drill ran out of power, and I had to use a hand drill for the other 120! My arms got so tired, I thought they'd fall off!

But the hard work wasn't over yet. The spiles still had to be hammered into the holes. After we'd hammered away for what seemed like hours, I tasted the sap that was seeping from the spiles. It was so watery, I wondered if we'd ever be able to turn it into syrup.

Maple sap flows on mild days after very cold nights. That night there was a frost, and the next morning dawned bright and sunny. I rushed out to peer into the nearest pail, but was I disappointed. The pail was nearly empty, and what there was in the bottom was frozen.

But by 10 a.m. the sun had warmed the tree roots, and I started to hear the *plink, plink* of sap dripping into pails all over the bush. At 11:30 a.m. I started pouring the sap into a huge sap barrel. It takes 40 L of sap to make just 1 L of syrup. The sap barrel is so large, my uncle's father used horses to haul it. I like that idea, but Uncle Dave prefers snowmobiles.

While I was collecting sap, Uncle Dave started a roaring fire in the evaporator — a furnace-like stove where the sap is boiled until most of the

water has evaporated. What's left is syrup.

What I remember most about the next part is the heat, the smoke, the watery eyes, and the waiting. All afternoon I stoked the fire and watched the level of the sap go down. I was sure there'd soon be none left.

Finally, my uncle poured some of the sap into a tall cylinder. Then he dropped in a float shaped a bit like a thermometer. It floated at the red "syrup" line. "We've done it, Uncle Dave," I shouted. "Maple syrup."

Carefully, Uncle Dave and I carried the syrup pan into the cabin and emptied it into a felt filter. This filter traps sediment called "sugar sand" — minerals the tree would normally use for food. Soon the syrup was cool enough to taste.

Was it worth all that work? You bet! I took some home, and we had pancakes and maple syrup every day for a week. When we got tired of pancakes, we had maple syrup on all sorts of other foods. In fact, just about the only thing I didn't try it on was hamburgers. Mmmm, maybe that's not such a bad idea.

Mark Mason as told to Helen Mason

Fritters

Have you ever boiled sap to make your own maple syrup?
Have you ever visited a sugar bush and bought some of the
freshly made "liquid gold"? Or do you buy it in tins or bottles at
a grocery store or a supermarket? Wherever your syrup comes
from, it will taste delicious poured over these Canadian apple
fritters!

You will need:

3 big apples	2 mL salt
250 mL flour	30 mL sugar
5 mL baking powder	1 egg
	250 mL milk

1. Peel the apples and remove the cores. Careful! Don't break the apples! Slice them about 5 mm thick.

2. Sift the flour and baking powder together.

3. In a bowl, beat the egg. Add the sugar and salt and beat some more.

4. Mix in a bit of the milk, then some of the flour mixture. Do this until they are all used up, and the batter is smooth and creamy.

5. Dip the apple slices in the batter.

6. Fry them in butter until they are golden brown all over.

Serve the apple fritters with maple syrup for an early spring treat.

Barbara Rennick

UNIT 4
Bullfrogs and Peepers

Five Little Frogs

Music by Virginia Pavelko
Words by Louise Binder Scott

Five green   and speck-led frogs   sat on   a speck-led log,

Eat-ing   some most de - li - cious bugs. *(yum yum)*

One jumped   in - to   the pool, where it   was nice and cool,

Then there   were four green speck-led   frogs. *(gllb, gllb)*

2nd verse: Four green and speckled frogs . . . .
3rd verse: Three green and speckled frogs . . . .
4th verse: Two green and speckled frogs . . . .
5th verse: One green and speckled frog . . . no green speckled frogs.

The Exploding Frog

An ox came to drink some water at a pond. The frogs, sitting on lily pads, saw how gigantic the ox was and were stunned. "Bigger than the trees," they said to one another after the ox left. "Bigger than the sky."

Later in the day, when the oldest frog finally rose from his sleep, they were still chattering about the size of the ox. The oldest frog asked sharply, "What is all this talk about the size of an ox? I myself can be bigger than any ox."

"But," said the other frogs, "that ox was *really* big."

"I've heard enough of this business," said the oldest frog. He took a deep breath and expanded to twice his original size. "See how big I am — as big as an ox for sure," he gloated.

"No, not quite that big," croaked the smaller frogs.

"One more breath should do it then," he said, and grew twice as large again.

"Oh," said the frogs, "this *is* amazing, but the ox was far larger."

Then, because the frog hated to be bested at anything, he took a third breath. But, as all the other frogs stared at his even greater size, he suddenly exploded.

"He was getting there all right," they said sadly. "But he would never have been as big as he wanted."

John McFarland

Bullfrogs and Peepers

"Ribbet!" "Jug-o'-rum!" "Eee-EEEEP!" Every spring the air is filled with the sound of frogs as they come out of hibernation. They've spent the winter sleeping under logs or stones or buried in mud. Now it is time to gather together near ponds and quiet streams where the females will lay their eggs.

There are actually many different kinds and sizes of frogs. The largest is the bullfrog which can grow as long as fifteen centimetres. The spring peeper, by comparison, is very tiny. It is only about three centimetres long when fully grown. That's about the difference in size between the whole length of a human hand and the first joint of the thumb.

The bullfrog is usually found near lakes and streams. Both males and females are a dull green colour except for their throats and bellies which are pale grey. They have huge, bulging eyes and powerful, webbed hind feet. The males also have a vocal sac or pouch under their jaws. They fill this pouch with air, like a balloon, and then let it out quickly to give the characteristic call "Jug-o'-rum!"

In spring the female bullfrogs lay their eggs in a mass on the surface of the water. They sometimes lay over twenty thousand eggs, all held together in long chains of transparent jelly. You can see the eggs inside which look like black dots. But they grow quickly in the hot sun and are hatched within three weeks.

The creatures that are hatched do not look at all like bullfrogs. They look more like big, round heads with a tail attached. These larvae, or tadpoles as you may know them, have gills and a tail instead of lungs and legs. This means that they can't live on land as their parents do. Instead, they swim about in the water like fish.

It takes bullfrog tadpoles a long time to grow lungs and legs. In fact, they have to wait for two whole years before the change, or metamorphosis, is finished. Only after their second winter of hibernation are they able to live on land, call out

"Jug-o'-rum," and lay eggs to start a new generation.

Spring peepers are quite different from bullfrogs. You can hear them in April and May near small pools of water where reeds or other plants grow. The males have vocal sacs like bullfrogs. But because they are so tiny, their call sounds more like a shrill whistle, "Eee-EEEEP!"

Spring peepers range in colour from light brown to olive grey. Their backs are decorated with an "X" made by two dark brown stripes. Spring peepers also have special pads on their toes to help them climb. These work like suction cups as they crawl up reeds, bushes, and even trees.

In spring the female lays almost a thousand eggs. However, she does this one at a time instead of in a mass. To protect the eggs, she attaches each one to a reed or plant underwater. The eggs stay there for one to two weeks until they are hatched some time in June.

Like bullfrogs, spring peepers start out as tadpoles. But metamorphosis takes place much more quickly. Within three months, the change is complete. The tadpoles have grown lungs and legs and are full-sized spring peepers. They join their parents on land and prepare to spend their first winter hibernating under rocks or leaves or fallen trees.

Gillian Bartlett

Frog Music

In a boggy old bog
by a loggy old log
sat a froggy old frog.

He had spots on his skin;
on his face was a grin
that was wide and was thin.

He was green. He was fat
as an old Cheshire cat.
He was flat where he sat.

While he hoped that a fly
would fly by by-and-by,

it was also his wish
to avoid Mr. Fish,

Mr. Turtle, and tall
Mr. Heron, since all
of them *might* pay a call,

and just *might* be aware
of his grin, skin, and bare

bulgy head, and those eyes,
very goggly in size.

So he grinned and just sat,
sat and sat, sat and sat,
looking silly like that.

But no fish saw him grin,
thinking, *Now* he'll jump in!

and no turtle a-cruise
thought him there in the ooze,

as a heron on one
leggy leg would have done.
Not a twitch in him — none.

Isn't life pretty grim
for a frog? Think of him.

But then think of that fly
flying by by-and-by.

David McCord

The Frog

Crak-ak!
Where is he?
I hear him singing over there — or is he over *there?*
Crak-ak!
If I tip-toe softly towards his voice, I may see him.

So I walk gently over the damp grass,
Following his
Crak-ak!

Is he by the fence?
— Or is it just a root.
Crak-ak!
Is he there in the long grass?
No.
That is just a stone.

Where is he?
He is too well hidden for me to see with my untrained eye.
Oh well,
I have other things to do.

And as I walk away,
He laughs.
Crak-ak!

       Joyce Pullen

The Strange Story of the Frog Who Became a Prince

Many years ago there was a handsome frog who lived by a rather nice pond. He had fun all day, and at night he had happy dreams. Every day was exactly the same as every other day.

He liked to swim in the pond and hop in the grass. He hopped high and he hopped low. When he was feeling silly he hopped sideways. In the grass and in the pond, the handsome frog found caterpillars, grasshoppers, and many other good things to eat.

His skin was green like the grass and brown like the pond and gold like the sun. He had black eyes which poked out on either side of his head. He was a very handsome frog indeed.

One day he was minding his own business, catching caterpillars and doing some rather fine hopping, when a wicked witch came swimming across the pond. She had a wet black hat and a wet black dress, and she had black eyes right on the front of her face. She looked like a bad dream.

But the handsome frog thought she looked rather interesting.
"Will you join me for a lunch of caterpillar?" he asked the
wicked witch, as he took a happy sideways jump. "I'd be happy
to cut mine in half."

"ICK!" said the wicked witch, making a face.

"What did you say?" he asked.

"People don't eat caterpillars," she said, making a face.
"ICK!"

The frog looked at the interesting witch who had a face like a
bad dream. "What do people eat if they don't eat caterpillars?"
he asked.

The witch put her hand into her big wet pocket and took out
a very soggy peanut butter sandwich. "Have some of this," she
said. "I'll share it with you. It's delicious." She broke the
sandwich in half and handed him a piece.

The frog bit into the sandwich. "ICK!" he said.

The wicked witch looked at the handsome frog. She smiled a wicked smile. Then she snapped her fingers and said:

ECNRP!

which sounded like a hiccup but which is really PRINCE spelled backwards.

Instantly the handsome frog turned into a prince.

"What have you done to me?" he asked.

"I've changed you into a prince," she said. "Aren't I clever?"

"But why?" he asked.

"Because I wanted to," she said.

He looked at his pink skin and felt his big ears and the hair on his round head. "My skin is as smooth as a worm, and my ears are like leaves, and my head has grass growing on it!" he cried. "Please change me back into the handsome frog I used to be."

The wicked witch smiled. "Oh, I can't do that," she said. "I don't remember how."

"Why, oh why did you do such a careless thing?" the prince asked, weeping. "I was such a handsome, happy frog, and then along you came and turned me into an ugly prince."

The wicked witch said, "I wanted to see if I could still do magic. Many years ago I changed a handsome prince into an ugly frog. What a good trick *that* was! But he was unhappy too. People are so unadventurous. Did you ever hear of him?"

"Indeed I did," said the prince. "They say he cried all day and frightened the polliwogs with all that talk about witches.

They say he was a very low hopper and a slow swimmer as well. When he disappeared, everyone said he had been changed back into a prince. Now, how did you do *that*?"

The witch shrugged. "Who can remember? It was years and years ago."

"Try to remember," said the prince.

"It was all part of a magic spell I've forgotten."

The prince said, "What was that magic word you said when you changed me into a prince?"

"I said PRINCE backwards," she said. "Some magic spells work that way. You have to keep trying new words because some work and some don't, although I've never known why."

"Well, try saying that one again," said the prince.

$$ECNIRP!$$

said the witch loudly.

Nothing happened.

"Try FROG backwards," said the prince.

"GORF!" said the witch.

"Try WATER."

"RETAW!"

"Try SUN."

"NUS!"

"Try GRASS."

"SSARG," she hissed.

The prince thought hard and then said softly, "Try MAGIC WORD."

"What a good idea," said the witch. "CIGAM DROW!"

Nothing happened. The prince sat down in the tall grass and began to cry again, more loudly than before.

"Now stop that," said the witch. "I don't know if you know this, but anyone would rather be a prince than a frog."

"Really?" asked the prince. "Why?"

The witch thought hard for a moment, and then she said, "Well, for one thing, you can have a name when you're a person. A name tells people who you are. Pick any name you like, and it will be yours. How about a fine name like TOM?"

"TOM?" said the prince. "Is that a name? It sounds like something falling in the grass at night when it's dark."

"How about HARRY?" asked the witch.

"Is *that* a name?" asked the prince. "It sounds like a cricket calling."

"What about a noble, princely French name like ALPHONSE?" asked the witch.

"It sounds like a beaver sneezing," said the prince.

"You really are a difficult person to please," said the witch. "Look at your nice clothes. Clothes keep you warm and make you look nice."

"Warm!" said the prince. "My legs are strangling. I'm boiling. I can hardly jump."

"Only necks can strangle," said the witch. "Only water can boil. Only frogs and horses and grasshoppers jump around in that boring way. And furthermore," said the witch, "people can learn how to read." She took a wet newspaper out of her wet pocket. "You see, these are words," she said. "Look, this word says 'pond.'"

"Pond?" he said. "It doesn't look like a pond at all. It looks just like muddy hummingbird footprints."

"How old are you anyhow?" said the witch.

"I was born in the spring," said the frog.

"Well, no wonder," said the witch. "You can't learn to read until you're six years old. I'm very sorry, but I don't know how to break the spell," said the witch, a little crabby now. "You'll just have to learn to like being a prince. Come now, I'll teach you how to whistle and snap your fingers. Now *there* are two things no frog can do."

The witch whistled "Row, Row, Row Your Boat" for the prince. The prince tried and tried, but he could not whistle.

"Why would anyone want to whistle or snap his fingers anyhow?" asked the prince.

"Whistling is a very useful trick," said the witch. "You can call your dog when you whistle."

"I hate dogs," said the prince.

"Well, never mind," said the witch. "I'll teach you how to snap your fingers."

The witch snapped her fingers. And suddenly she remembered. She remembered that she had not snapped her fingers when she said her magic words backwards.

She leaned closer to the poor unhappy prince, looked into his sad eyes, snapped her fingers, and said:

CIGAM ᴅROW!

"I feel different!" said the prince.

"Why, look what I've done!" said the witch. "I've changed you into a beautiful princess! How charming!"

"HOW EMBARRASSING!" said the princess who used to be a prince who used to be a frog. "Keep trying, please. I think you're on the right track."

SSARG!

said the witch, snapping her fingers. And the princess who used to be a prince who used to be a frog changed again.

"You're getting warmer," said the centaur who used to be a princess who used to be a prince who used to be a frog.

The witch snapped her fingers again and said:

NUS! RETAW!

The merman who used to be a centaur who used to be a princess who used to be a prince who used to be a frog said, "Almost, but not quite. Try again."

The witch snapped her fingers very loudly twice and cried:

GORF, GORF!

And the spell was broken.

The handsome frog was very happy. He looked at himself in the pond, and he hopped high, and he hopped low. Then he hopped sideways. He swam across the pond and back. He ate a caterpillar.

"If you change your mind and want to be a prince again, just call me," said the witch, as she put on her swimming goggles.

"Oh, no!" said the frog. "But if I meet someone else who would like to be changed into a prince, how do I find you?"

"Just whistle or snap your fingers, and I'll be there," said the witch, as she jumped into the pond and swam away.

The handsome frog laughed. He laughed and laughed until he was very tired. Then he sat down on a warm rock and told the whole story to a tree toad, who didn't believe it.

Elinor Lander Horwitz

Something More:

I Believe in Unicorns

Once there was a Unicorn. He was born one crisp winter's night, leaping from a fiery volcano.

On the same night, in the far North, a little boy, with blue eyes, leaped from his mother and was tossed into this world. His father, who fished in the great waters off the coast, was glad. He had a son now who one day would help him pull in the nets.

The Unicorn grew lonely. He had no family except the wind, no brothers or sisters except the bright stars, no friends except the wild creatures, but they disdained him, for he was not like them.

Raif was lonely, too. His father was often away fishing, and his mother worked all day in the fields, so Raif played alone with only birdsong for company. He listened to the falcon's kreen and watched silently as the Arctic fox and her cubs slipped from their lair.

One day he found a dried-out tree root. It was smooth and beautiful to him, like a Unicorn. He kept it, and at night he dreamed of being small enough to gallop through his bedroom window and make a journey to the stars.

The Unicorn travelled the world. His hooves beat out magical rhymes on a thousand roof-tops. The music of his heels touched echoes in a million hearts, but people did not recognize him nor the songs which he sang. But Raif heard his roar. Raif threw open his window. He gazed at the stars.

"Father," he asked, "does the Unicorn live in the sky?"

"No," his father replied, closing the window, "it's only a traveller's tale."

Raif sighed as he got into bed, but in his dreams he rode his magic Unicorn all over the skies. The Unicorn drew near on silent feet and stared longingly at the sleeping boy, and in the morning Raif saw where his breath had frozen on the window pane.

Shaking his mane like sea-foam, the Unicorn wept tears of flame, for humans no longer believed in him. The light faded from his horn. Each time he stopped in the path of a traveller who turned his eyes away, each time he passed by a lighted window which was shut against him, each time a father laughed at his name — the Unicorn grew more transparent, his coat turned to ashes, his flesh wore away.

One day Raif's mother fell ill and had to stay in bed. Raif was not big enough to help her in the fields. He could not do her work. Her eyes and hungry cheeks made him tremble. Raif took her cold hand in his and told her about his dreams of the wonderful Unicorn.

"I've seen him," he said, "and heard him sing, and there's magic in him that makes people better, if only they believe in him hard enough."

There were tears in his mother's eyes as she shook her head, but she smiled at her son and kissed him.

That night Raif stared out the window. He felt very sleepy. At last a whisper crept from his throat: "Doesn't the Unicorn live any more? Doesn't he?"

His heart grew heavier, for the wind seemed to blow the words back in his face.

It was close to dawn. The Unicorn, with weariness deep in his bones, paused for breath on an ice-floe travelling to the ocean. A light shone from a lonely cabin, and the Unicorn felt faintly the pull of a human sadness. He saw a small boy wandering towards the dark woods. Quietly he approached. Closer came the Unicorn until the warm breath from his nostrils touched Raif's cheek.

Raif looked up but saw nothing. Suddenly he cried, "They're wrong! They're wrong! I dreamed of him, and his songs put the leap into the lame!" He took out his knife and began to carve the letters on the trunk of a tree, whispering the words softly to himself as he worked:

I BELIEVE IN UNICORNS

Light sprang from the Unicorn's horn, filling the place with a warm glow.

Raif leaped round. "It's true!" he cried. "I knew it was true!"

"Which was why you saw me," said the Unicorn, and neighed proudly.

The Unicorn bore Raif up, high and swift as the east wind. Below, Raif's mother breathed deeply as her fever departed. And at the windows of a thousand sleeping children, Raif cried out:

> "The Unicorn last of them all was here,
> Remember his name or he'll disappear.
> When you stare at the stars
> Through your mind's magic door,
> You'll KNOW when you hear
> The UNICORN'S roar!"

Adam John Munthe

Acknowledgements

Page 8: "The Longest Journey in the World" by Michael Rosen from **You Can't Catch Me.** Published by Andre Deutsch. Also published in **A Second Poetry Book** compiled by John Foster, Oxford University Press, 1980.

Page 12: From **The Climb** by Carol Carrick. Text copyright © 1980 by Carol Carrick. Reprinted by permission of Clarion Books, a Houghton Mifflin Company.

Page 28: Excerpt from **Anna, Grandpa, and the Big Storm** by Carla Stevens. Copyright © 1982 by Carla Stevens. Reprinted by permission of Clarion Books/Ticknor & Fields, a Houghton Mifflin Company.

Pages 36, 76: "Snow Today," originally called "November," and "I'm glad I don't live" by Fran Newman from **Sunflakes and Snowshine** by Fran Newman and Claudette Boulanger. Reprinted by permission of Scholastic-TAB Publications, Ltd.

Page 38: "This Cat" in **Dogs & Dragons, Trees & Dreams:** A Collection of Poems by Karla Kuskin. Copyright © 1975 by Karla Kuskin. By permission of Harper & Row, Publishers, Inc.

Page 39: "Jenny's Adopted Brothers" from **Jenny and the Cat Club** by Esther Averill. Copyright 1952, 1973 by Esther Averill. Reprinted by permission of Harper & Row, Publishers, Inc.

Page 46: "Tabitha Twitchell" by Jean Conder Soule from Kits, Cats, Lions & Tigers selected by Lee Bennett Hopkins. Reprinted by permission of the author.

Page 50: "The Climbing Cat" by Margaret Coe. © W.J. Gage Limited 1963. From **Nunny Bag 2.** Reprinted by permission of Gage Publishing Limited.

Page 63: "Chang McTang McQuarter Cat" from **You Read to Me, I'll Read to You** by John Ciardi, illustrated by Edward Gorey (J.B. Lippincott Co.). Copyright © 1962 by John Ciardi. By permission of Harper & Row, Publishers, Inc.

Page 66: Text adapted from Betty Waterton, **Pettranella.** Copyright © 1980 Betty Waterton. Reprinted by permission of Douglas & McIntyre Ltd., Vancouver.

Page 78: "Sugaring Off" by Helen Guiton. © W.J. Gage Limited, 1964. From **Nunny Bag 3.** Reprinted by permission of Gage Publishing Limited.

Page 80: "Liquid Gold" by Mark Mason as told to Helen Mason. Reprinted from **Owl Magazine** with permission of the publisher, The Young Naturalist Foundation.

Page 83: "Fritters" by Barbara Rennick. Used by permission of the author.